Warm Corners

Warm Corners

Poems by

May Morris, Fiona McIlroy, Deb Foskey and Fran McIlroy

Acknowledgements

Some of these poems have appeared previously:
'Arrest' – *Social Alternatives*; 'Sublime to the ridiculous' – *Canberra Times*;
'Cabanandra' – *Blast*; 'Teacher at the Year 10 formal' – *Redoubt*;
'Baghdad Nights 16.1.91' – *Mothers and Others for Peace*.

Warm Corners
ISBN 978 1 74027 127 1
Copyright © text Cecily McIlroy, Fiona McIlroy,
Deb Foskey and Fran McIlroy 2002
Copyright © cover photo 'The hut' Samara McIlroy
(previously published on the cover of Photoaccess)

This collection first published 2002
Reprinted 2019

GINNINDERRA PRESS
PO Box 3461 Port Adelaide 5015
www.ginninderrapress.com.au

Contents

Preface	7
May Morris	9
November in Tuross Head	9
Grey Power	10
Tea and Scones	11
One-dimensional	12
Cats	13
Forties Girls	14
Playing Happy Families	15
Arrest	16
To Eleni – Almost Three	17
Vaucluse Bus	18
Her Story	19
Peace Conference	20
Yuletide	21
Three Friends	22
Pink Slip	23
Poets as Fringe-dwellers	24
Born Again	25
Time Travellers	26
Some of the Following Scenes May Offend	27
Autumn	28
Anthropologically speaking	29
Inquest	30
Rwanda Report	31
Propitiation	32
Fiona McIlroy	33
For Cecily	33
Sublime to the ridiculous	34

Between the lines	36
There it is, in black and white	37
Monaro drought from the air	40
Relationship	42
Milmilay	43
Chill wind	45
Night canter	46
Cabanandra	47
Singing stones	48
Body politic	50
Motherhood	51
Deb Foskey	**52**
Early love	52
Feeling good	53
The baby's a month old	54
Winter Moon	55
another poem on this productive day	56
Teacher at the Year 10 formal	57
A message to the Very Deep	58
The singing tapestry	59
Holy connections	60
Baghdad Night 16.1.91	61
Fran McIlroy	**63**
Seven Mile Beach	63
Friday	65
Rain at Kangaroo Island	66
Buckets	68
Baby Before, Santa Now	69

Preface

The authors chose the title *Warm Corners* with a surprising consensus. It suggests several aspects of their connectedness. Their shared history at 'Warm Corners' is a good starting point. On another level, the title reflects the different paths taken by each, yet relationship gives warmth to their lives. The cover photo depicts a shaft of morning light parting the smoke, and a kettle for the eternal conversations over a cup of tea in a cosy corner.

At the top of a dirt track leading to the Jingalalla River, a sign points to the Warm Corners Track. The track is named after the Warm Corners Creek, which feeds the Jingalalla.

Nestled in the foothills of the Monaro tablelands, locals referred to Warm Corners as 'stinking hot. You grow good tomatoes down there. Bushfire country.' Others have been known to comment, 'Warm Corners, eh? You mean Cold Corners. Bloody cold down there on the creek. Freezes over.' Both descriptions fit, since the area is marked by extreme weather swings; sudden shifts of mood. Then there is the warm fuzzy take. When the British conservationist David Bellamy stayed the night at Warm Corners, he left a card saying, 'The Warm Corners of the world are safe with people like you.'

Like the tributaries of the Jingalalla River, the women who wrote this book are closely linked, but very different. *Warm Corners* reflects an inner landscape that is rich in texture and mood. The women have travelled through many of life's passages and rites, shared beginnings and endings, and known love and loss. They now live in different places, but remain close friends. Writing is a strong connecting thread.

The Warm Corners Women, 2002

May Morris

November in Tuross Head

Here in this ambiguous meeting place of sea and land
new houses grow like scabs on rocky headlands;
and where the black tribes camped and feasted
we live, tentative, in our squares and rectangles.

We preserve life at any cost,
tend our gardens, walk miles, take our heart pills
    and herbal teas
and recreate ourselves at golf and bingo;
we are pale exiles rooted in far-off countries.

And here
scarlet rosellas gossip in silken voices –
they wear party gear every day, the red and the blue.
Galahs in more sober pinks and greys
hang on the high wires, courtesy of the county council.
And here's a crowded tree all rainbow-coloured
The lorikeets are back, looking for honeyed blossom
scattering scarlet under my banksia tree.

Tonight the moon's half-full
hidden under cloud; the waves crash
against the obdurate cliffs. We hear
the ancient battle between the sea and land
as the southerly sweeps in.

Grey Power

On fine blue mornings you'll see them
by the paper shop, the post office,
the Mower Men greet each other
G'day, mate, great match. How's Madge (or Gwen or Molly)?
Their eyes swivel and they look away.

Madge (or Gwen or Molly)
is away at the daughter's, been gone a week
but they do not say they're lonely
and she may not be back.
For the old men know they're dull company
compared with a needy daughter
and a new grandson.

Their eyes swivel and they look away
into a future minus Madge
(or Gwen or Molly) perhaps forever. So
the new grass must fall
and the blue day must die,
killed by the roaring whine
of the Motor Mower Men.

Tea and Scones

There's a celebration of women's work
Patriotism and the Old Values
at the country hall.

Here you will see
crochet, knitwear
and every sort of embroidery
while the comfort of tea and scones
is taken under the Queen's gaze –
she looks a real picture up there on the wall.

The names on the honour board shine,
with new gold paint; but sixty years is a long time
and the Smiths, Browns and Robinsons may well have died
on life's battlefield.

Still, we remember them
at the going down of the sun
and the close
of yet another successful exhibition of work
by the CWA.

One-dimensional

Shadowy faces,
uncentred and flickering thoughts
behind the casual conversation around the barbecue.
Here we are safe
ensconced in our intellectual rightness.
Assumptions of unshakeable logic –
I think, therefore I am –
can it be otherwise?

I fear the closed compartments of the mind
the fenced-in thoughts, conclusions
propounded and proved,
the stunted action, the bitter and poisonous fruit
of the one-dimensional intellect.

Cats

Cats
like babies
birdsongs
good smells and other commonplace occurrences and delights
have little or no market value.

I gather her deathly love-gifts,
a chewed rat, a bright feather;
she's all purrs
        paws
                fur
                        claws
her delicate devotion reminding me
of my sanitary, supermarket mentality.

Forties Girls

For the camera
we wore lipsticked smiles
teetering on high heels
our poses as impermanent as our opinions.

We worried our seams weren't straight
our slips showing;
confusions revealed
uncertainties made visible.

Playing Happy Families

Once there was a family
went smoothly enough –
cogs meshed, engine ticked over.
Mothers were of course mothers;
fathers sometimes turned into fathers.

Things didn't last. Cogs slipped,
gears jammed, someone threw spanners.

We were just doing the fifties thing,
rearing the baby boomers generation.

Arrest

I think that death, when it comes, will take me by surprise
grabbing me by the arm, saying what's this,
what's this, catching me in the natural act of living.

Catching me out and sweeping me away
on a dark tide of discontinuity.

To Eleni – Almost Three

Eleni's kneeling on her chair,
spoon at the ready, waving.
I'm 'ungry, she cries, I'm 'ungry.
It's breakfast;
she's slurping up her cornflakes,
she's waving her spoon;
her flag's flying, she's moving,
moving on
moving…

Vaucluse Bus

Their words fall weightless, small hail
melting at once on patterned silk laps.

We pass clipped lawns, rose gardens
marching in line. Good solid brick
sheltering low-risk lives.

Under their patter fears hide
as eyes turn to storm-grey seas.
Change coming.

Her Story

Over decades
we've tramped in city streets
making exhibitions of ourselves
under banners.
We've scaled walls
we've upset applecarts
and spilt the beans.

We've marched for peace
and repealed abortion laws;
we've stopped wars
and uranium mining;
we've saved whales
and saved forests,
showing our colours.

We've sung our hopes
and shown our strength;
declared our beliefs
and worn utopias
like rainbow garments.

Peace Conference

Flashing a nervous neon smile
the organiser introduces the first speaker
in a line-up of notables.
We sit straight in our seats in obedient rows.
Will there be prizes for not interrupting?
Or refraining from
    groaning
        praying
            crying
laughing in the wrong places,
or just a cup of tea at playtime?

Two and a half million dollars spent on armaments every minute –
what was the proportion of trained scientists
working on defence worldwide?

Will Evil triumph over Good,
the unworthy over the worthy
if I forget the exact number
of people dying of starvation worldwide
but only remember their agony?

Should I give all my money to the peace movement
or just forgo my lunch?
And will I ever forgive myself
for joy at the newly opened rose
and the taste of the first apricot?

Yuletide

Relatives are plentiful
this time of the year.
Old photos also abound.

In that one, I look glamorous
and bemused;
you wore a moustache;
we were well turned-out in those days.

Sad, really, hanging on
in daily expectation
of the rose-strewn path of happiness.
It might have been like that
at that age – joy could always happen tomorrow.

Grey hair makes similar
that which was once distinctive.
I suppose old age is a sort of disguise.

After the season's greetings and the plum pudding
is perhaps the long flatness of age –
depends on the point of view.
Then
the faint clash of false teeth on false teeth
dry cheek on dry cheek
and unregretted goodbyes.

Three Friends

They swam in the Snowy that weekend,
bathing belles with greying hair;
not a media event, there were no cameras;
only the stiff pines and indomitable granite,
a kookaburra or two, some wood ducks,
could be called as witnesses.

Three wise witches
three ageing witches
shared their laughter and sorrows
swimming in the river
sitting by the river
worshipping the river.

At evening the currawongs and possums
shared supper with them by the campfire
while they sorted out the world.

Pink Slip

So what if there is a rattle or two,
maybe a weakness in the chassis;
gaps in the upholstery, stuffing leaking out?
Isn't that only a little rust,
not a sign of fatal decay?
Shall I speak of the fading spark,
or the chug chug of the starter
when there's frost about, and a westerly
blows icy from the mountains?
In short, can I keep the old heap
going for one more trip,
and will I try to qualify
once more for my pink slip?

Poets as Fringe-dwellers

Hard to find out if there are many of us;
we don't like standing up to be counted.
Subterranean folk, we peer out
hoping only not to be noticed.

We are the freaks of history, clawing at our boundaries;
sometimes we are also the future,
learning, perhaps too late, to be,
society's disabled relatives staying out of sight.

The rootless are born and made,
live like spiders in suspension
by a fine thread. Sometimes giddy
and very near to falling
we are unskilled tightrope walkers, knowing only
not to look down.

Born Again

I won't have to cut my toenails
when I'm dead
nor wash my hair and clothes
nor make my bed;
nor grieve for friends in pain
nor fret
about the dying forests
or the nuclear threat.

Will I miss my little comforts –
a cup of tea,
the sun's warmth, chatter of birds,
and the blue, blue sea?

And will I be reborn as a whale
or just a flea;
or a whiskery crustacean
from the watery creation
or a new, improved variety
of a Me?

Time Travellers

Travelling south, our train's a sinuous snake
balanced between the sea and the high cliffs –
sandstone rows of furred and broken teeth.
This is the pensioners' train; the talk's long and slow;
faces of old acquaintance
jostle the corridors of our memories.
We're past Wollongong and Kembla's a distant smudge.
Look! Albion Park's come out in mustard yellow;
the westerly's flattened the expensive ears of racehorses
and Kiama's waves are edged with a white frill.

Some of the Following Scenes May Offend

Who are those figures running across our screen?
Collapsed bodies, collapsed buildings, a television drama.
Why are these men dolled up in army gear, pointing guns?
Are they the baddies? No, they look like us, our sons, our husbands.
Just ordinary.

Why is that kid crying? Where's the mother?
Is that her lying there, a bloodied heap?
Oh, they're trying to capture a city.
But what's the use
of a destroyed city
and the people all gone?
This movie's got no plot that I can see.

Autumn

In this quiet June weather
the last yellow quince forgets to fall
(brown wrens skittering over the grass)
while men in dark suits with briefcases and economics degrees
doctor the economy,
other men with cracked smiles on TV screens
offer utopias
watch opinion polls
and give tax concessions to millionaires.

In South Africa, coffins are lowered daily into the dull earth;
in Europe after Chernobyl mothers give their children iodine tablets;
politicians offer reassurances;
and God has taken her sleeping bag, a tent and a good supply of kleenex
and joined the women's camp at Greenham Common.

Anthropologically speaking

Evelyn Reed
has a theory. Indeed
she believes that the female,
that great initiator,
fished a male from the primeval slime,
stood him upright, hosed him down
and told him to stay in the farmyard
with the other wild animals she had tamed
until he had learnt some table manners.

Inquest

A row of grey suits in a stuffy room;
the handmaiden to the coroner
bangs the door; fetches; carries; smiles;
it's better than the dole
to laugh at judgemental humour.
Death's all in a day's work to her.

So where's the blame? Here we have some heroes
but most are fools, fearful for their position,
for the glass of vintage wine at dinner;
the prized invitation; perhaps
the name on the honours list.

So they must bow and smile
and pass the ball on to the proper quarter.
Not here! Not me! The death curse is too heavy.
Besides, my department's badly understaffed
and saving lives takes time. And time is money.

Rwanda Report

Men of goodwill are looking at the holocaust
showing astonishment   shock   outrage.
Men of goodwill are surprised by the holocaust –
they rush bravely into the chaos
performing great deeds of rescue
after the event;
restoring life and the capacity
for continued suffering.

Have they laid their own ghosts,
their lurking fears of each other?

Women from the four corners of the world
are not amazed, seeing violence and death as everyday things,
knowing the machete   the gun   the fist
are not to be wondered at; knowing
that where there are weapons and men
there may be danger   pain   rape   death.

In Brisbane, Ballarat, Berlin,
in Moscow, Paris, Tigale,
they must snatch up their children
and run.

And the guns are exchanged
from nation to nation
for money and power.

No
the women are not amazed.

Propitiation

In the end, we had to forgive her her illness
her sudden disappearance into hospital;
    her operation
        her suffering
            the doctors
                the nurses
                    the technicians
                      the tests
                          the pills
                              the wasting body
                                  the homecoming.

We had to forgive her our fears
of our own illness
our own death.

Now we visit regularly,
bearing gifts and votive offerings.

Fiona McIlroy

For Cecily

From the living room
  a piccolo poem
    each shy note
      threads its way home
        through clouds of tone-deaf
          lopsided conversation

to circle your arms
  bracelet your wrists
    your deft and uncomplaining
      wrists at the wheel
        that seek to shake off
          the insistent clinging
            of history, gender and dishonesty

to display the true unyielding
  voice of the clay

Sublime to the ridiculous

Found

three relics
of a consumer age
fallen from Grace
Brothers, Coles,
K Mart, Woolworths,
from some hall of idol
worship

where worth is measured in dollars
and cool, hard business sense

Fallen, or were they thrown,
into Lake Ginninderra,
trinkets, or keepsakes
from Belconnen Mall

Three shopping trolleys
on their sides
ungainly shining icons
of our genocidal tribe

Heavy Metal
elemental
objets d'art

quintessential
Antipodes

Two hundred short
years compressed
her resources shorn
her clothing torn
to reveal her naked
clavicle

Here lies witness
to our gluttonous history
booty piled high
weaving wildly
down the aisle

Between the lines

cross-hatching cross-hatching
never could do cross-hatching

after sketching in the outline
of the thing
I was always left in doubt
as a child
where the light and shade occurred
where the secret behind the word
could hide
under the skin
the dark intent

I did bruise easily –
being sent to Coventry
a common event
friends bent to each other's ear
whispering about my unguessed-at
social atrocities

yes, I could guess
but never bluff myself too well
that I knew what went on
between
the lines

There it is, in black and white

Snowy squatted with us
scratching in the dust
under the shade of a truck
in sleepy Katherine

*'Your whiteman education
no good
for blackman'*
(Snowy mimes
ripping up paper)

*'Paper tears
paper burns.'*
(lights up a fag)

*'Whiteman law change
not black law.*

Blackman law in the rocks.

*You say blow up the rocks, then what?
No. My law is in the air,
everywhere.'*

Snowy rolls his eyes around
then claps them on my soul:
a flickering in the shadow of the truck

Take a quick swig of the fizzy
orange drink he gives me,
gulp
splutter explode, stumble out into the bleaching
sunlight
gubba got it and how –
nearly choked on blackman law

Now, as I write
it is hard to pin down
the literal truth
of the spoken word
but if what he says is so
the law must hover between
these lines
shiver in the leaves of the trees
that fed these pages

From cave to condominium

our common ear inherits
the air waves

Can we whitemen
learn to listen to the wind
in the silence; can we discern
the never-written
dreamtime whisperings
there for those who wish to
wake from the coded sleep
of literacy

*My law is in the air
everywhere*

Left with these skeletal words
have I stripped the sinew off
the ribs of truth
only to obscure the issue?

Why is the bird of abstraction
so inert? Why does the pinned
wing sting the eye?

Here it is, in black and white,
Snowy's law as tort
elusive
as the sip of fizzy drink
caught in the throat

Monaro drought from the air

Monaro Plateau
crumpled-paper tableau
some inhibited adult
scratched on it with pen
smearing paint on thin
leaving patches bare

didn't dare
cover the whole thing
with colour
allow tones to mix
and match

Monaro's skin
old and thin
worn and wrinkled
cracked in the folds

on skulls of hills
and in her armpits
stubbly hair still shows
where it once grew dense
and profusely

the neck is shorn
in straight lines
fences blunting tendons
replacing curve with
certainty

naturally flat
bland areas

where eucalypts once
bent their wind-warped forms
waving their arms about

look unprepared
naked
bar the windows
dead black snakes
guarding a gardenless Eden

soon to be planted with
featureless uniform
fast-growing pinus radiata
neat well-cut

black dinner suit and tie
short back and sides
formal as hell

on the other side of the hill
still the rough tousled
casual look
the look
Australia likes to sell abroad

Relationship

I wanted to say things in sunlight
but today the world washed me clean
with thunderstorm
of ache for form and matter

was the sound of the birds after rain
a yawn as the gods prepared
the next wonder?

did the birds send sparks to enlighten
or just the splinters
from a fallen tree?

questions resting on premises
disappear when lightning strikes

so why the fear?

dead trees finger-pointing skyward
ask for it after all

these words still wet with recent squalls
refuse to jell

the word
must spell yet not reveal
that what we are is not
all there is to tell

Milmilay

my skinsister
Milmilay
smiling
conspiratorially

answering my awkward
queries
innocently
black eyes dancing
quick to sense a joke

provoking me to smile
at my own blunders in
cultural ineptitude

my black skinsister stepped
lightly by my side
as we walked down cement
stairs to bed
in airless dormitories

reeling from
cerebral conference
proceedings
you placed
your palm in mine
and made circles
with thumbs
our fingers entwined

when we said goodnight
you said, 'if you get any
objections at the office
when you visit Millingimbi
tell em Milmilay is your skinsister'

as I lay gazing
at the fan in my room
your name circled
in my mind
lay lightly like your palm
in my memory

Milmilay

Chill wind

some nights
a chill arrives
on the wind
and leaves behind
a lemon sky

the baby's bedtime
makes her cry
her bottle, my kiss
the wrong shape or size

I try to shake
the night by the arm
to warm the cot
to pour the milk
of human kindness
all around

but much too late
the night is soured
the colour of whey prevails
as the light fades

I must lie with
the sodden curd
of my bed
till day

Night canter

eyes rest soft on pillow
of horizon

slow and regular
hoofbeat on the brow
of the hill

suddenly –
a gate!

heartbeat rises to meet the now
brought up short before tomorrow

Cabanandra

we aim high
here in the foothills
of the Monaro
plateau

one slip of the tongue
travels too far

at night
our scalps prickle
with stars

Singing stones

Each of us owns
a dry creek-bed
crying out
for its singing stones

Take out the stitches
from old scar tissue
covering up
some painful issue

Unleash the tears
long locked inside
roll off the rock
let go the pride

Our psychic springs
will not run dry
if we choose to live
before we die

Neuronal pathways
ingrown, inbred
seal our hearts off
from our head

Mental mantras
now stone-dead
tell us to act on
what others have said

Each of us owns
a dry creek-bed
crying out for its
singing stones

Body politic

the feminine –
a wellspring
inside the iron heart
is gently
persistently
corroding its hollow
chambers

soon she will
pump new blood
through the arteries
of a robotic
body politic

Motherhood

never was much good
at deciding
which side the seam
should be sewn up
so darling
you'll have to grow
from seedhood
with no one providing
a trellis
or training your tendrils
to cling

no
it's not sewing
I'm good at
I'm afraid

but threading the needle

posing the question

knowing the tone
and texture
of a thing

drawing out
the beauty of a fabric

these I dedicate to you
in your seamless infancy

Deb Foskey

Early love

My window reflects
golden brown
on the wardrobe.

A sound outside:
I look to the sunlight.

I see trees
blank
I see grass
blank
two parked cars
blank
fence blank
shadows blank
sky blue
blank blank
gate blank.
I see all these things
but no you.
Blank.

Feeling good

Twinkling of star
was caught in my windscreen
when I looked out tonight.

The heavens gazed down:
infinity stared me in the eye.

I on my small planet
gazed up.

The heavens don't dwarf me;
the sky is just big enough
for me
to feel at home.

The baby's a month old

Rediscovering
the scope of being –

my shadow had a halo of golden light
as the river worked its magic.

I lay down on the grass
and brushed rabbit turds from my hair –

the middle of a honey day
and children sleeping.

Winter Moon

I'm light-headed with the winter moon
whose glow releases the spring in me
tonight.

The bush stirs,
rustles, pounds
as I pass.
I feel the crouch
of furred body nearby
but my indoor eyes
stare only into the black hole
of the shadows.

The naked manna gums
twist and turn,
bend and curve,
as the moon moulds
and shapes
licking at the bark
with phosphorescent tongue;
such sensuous fingers,
stroking the frost as it glistens and
gleams on the grass.

Ah, winter'd first full moon
of hard-edged roundness.
I drink up your glow,
soak my bones in your light.

another poem on this productive day

In this house the nights are busy.
Even before the people leave
to go to bed

the rats and mice are stirring in their paper beds.

The house, with its uninhabitable
people corners,
is the perfect penthouse
for smaller fry.

Nightly the rat trap
with its enticing delicacy
remains coiled,
untapped.

The cat dreams of lizards
in its sleep.

Teacher at the Year 10 formal

The sacrifice of the virgins,
twirling and sparkling,
spinning and shining:

I watch from the distance of years.
I see their tears fall
as they say a heartbroken farewell to
teachers they hardly know.
A chapter is closing.

Schooldays are the happiest days
of your life.

Doubtless
they never believed it.
But for a moment
they sense that
it might be true.

A message to the Very Deep

Dear mother,
as you lay dying,
I held your hand,
resisting the impulse to say
the words that roared in my heart.

So I whisper them now,
where brothers and nurses can't hear:

when you see my son,
say hello from me.

The singing tapestry

Surrounded by photos from the past
I am confronted by the Things that Matter.

There's nothing
from my political work.
People don't take photos
at meetings.

There are photos
of Bran and Dayo and Minya and Bob
on an early billy cart,
smiles all over their faces.
And one of Sam and Cec
in Cec's kitchen
that isn't Cec's
any more.

The past —
that rich tapestry of which I'm made.
It sings to me
in this bleak landscape
which will, one day,
be part of the picture.

Holy connections

I think of you
Mary, mother of a god,
as this time of the year comes around.

I wonder how you
were coping
two years past
the death of your son.

Were you standing
in a garden in winter
pulling out the dried
remnants of plants, so fruitful in summer,
whose season has passed,

wondering
for the seventy-first-zillionth time
if there is life beyond death
and if so, how,
what, why and oh where

and involved in the perilous struggle
of personal reconstruction?

Baghdad Night 16.1.91

It happened while the people slept
(but of course they did not sleep).
At four o'clock in the morning
the first birds were thinking about singing,
the sun will rise tomorrow.

Tossing and turning,
listening to the skies,
the children in the parents' bed –
doubt then reassurance,
the held breath.

The first plane swoops overhead
in a supersonic scream –
silence
broken by the sound of heartbeats,
clocks measuring mortality
so easily stopped.

We remember and remind ourselves
to breathe.

On this planet
we are all in this war
anticipating the shock waves
as the Earth is gouged
and blistered.

In one country,
women and children die
while in another,
people sit with iced drinks
watching the authorised TV version.

The war goes all night.
We cannot turn it off,
even in our sleep
(but of course we do not sleep).

Fran McIlroy

Seven Mile Beach

We catch sight of boundless
panorama skyline.
Rocky ledge to hazy mountain's edge,

line of sea, white breaking line,
our blue-green ocean
stretches across Earth's planet ball.

The clear sea swells, lolls, sheltering
lounging whales and mirroring
arc-winged gulls,

surf bends languorously
over core contours
to the melting season's ice.

Sensual lap, salty crash
wave slaps and swirls
at our breasts' curves.

We leap the spray
and swim steady tingling overarm
through bright refrigerated water,

run sandy gold-warm steps
to stand pleased, salt-cured, tangy,
sun towels our backs;

clatter home on thongs
to chatter, tea and toast
kiss the cup, flex the tanning muscle
    lazy swims and summer rays return.

Friday

Here in our city of quiet travellers
    wending our lives from toddler to 'timer
we crowd our bus
    hands and arms stretching
leaning and lurching
    to a driver's eye line,

inside each retina a memory laden
    with our life.
Our week of work sketches
    its branches into soft lit rest.
We dance a Saturday's promise
    leap the kerb of wages
    to a sandy shore of ease.

Rain at Kangaroo Island

Drought dries the ponds
    like an iconoclastic sponge.

Wizened river beds –
    old rocks crusted with
    mudpacks
hush to hear the fertilising
    raindrops
gentle mallee shower of
    weather
tendrils of wet red dust
    joining in a fractal-
    shaped embrace,
rain,
    to caress the burr
    and soften the fontanelle
    of infant newborn herbs.

Clay: slither to the left

Night: black power in tandem
    stillness
    with the solidarity beams
    of moon circle

    filling gravel spaces
    with rainy slants
    almost gurgling into
    running rivulets

almost wet.

Buckets

Buckets of drifting words on the page:
    just little peppercorns of thoughts
        some powdery some cracked some ground.

Lying in the arms of affection
    head resting, mind bobbing
thinking backwards about restlessness
    about kindness, about friends.

What a moonstruck adolescent
    to crave the confectioneries of life.
To laud them, to place the sweetness
    close to the invisible bustling corpuscles.
To inject my body with light, with
    miracle, with scent, with gratitude.

Thank you to the nurturing gifts of
    my writing friends.

To the unrepentant extrovert
    waggling her breasts in the
    picture window
    who runs to plant a genial kiss
    on the cheek of her departing lover.

Thank you to the animation that drums my fingers –
    warms the muscles,
    lifts the strokes of pen –
    beads the words on the paper thread.

Baby Before, Santa Now

From a tiny dot in the ever-expanding universe
    you were an adorable you, as a baby:
    with sweet chubby peachskin.
    You'd smile all the while and sing.
Then, toddler,
    you chattered in cheer
    and sang toy-soldier songs
    but hid the replica guns.
So compassionate a baby…

Now adult,
    hip to hip with your lover,
    you perform as cheerful Santa.
    Tall bending listener,
    upon you I heap praises.
You beam and bring the shine of
    Christmas-tinselled tree
    as you present bright parcels.

Your gift for craft,
    now tabled as an artist's palette feast,
    doubles as a chef's rainbowed banquet and
    the sculptor's tableau of chiselled wood.

Santa, newly captain of your ship,
    you are ready to slip the anchored past.
Place your strengthening grip upon your timber,
    take a compass bearing.
I see you are tall-masted to stride on, and lead.

www.ingramcontent.com/pod-product-compliance
Lightning Source LLC
Chambersburg PA
CBHW062154100526
44589CB00014B/1839